MALVERN
"HILL OF FOUNTAINS"

Ancient Origins, Beliefs and Superstitions surrounding
Wells and Well Dressing

by Rose Garrard

Drawings by Rose Garrard

In memor
a dedicated
Cornishman ai
my husband,
and companion fo
Kerry Marshal Trengove
1946-1991

GW00674533

Garrard Art Publications

www.garrardart.co.uk
publications@garrardart.co.uk

Garrard Art Publications

Design Layout by Rose Garrard

Well Dressing Photographs by Ray Roberts,
(unless otherwise credited)
Digital Production by Ray Roberts

Printed by Aspect Design, Malvern

ISBN 10: 1-905795-01-7
ISBN 13: 978-1-905795-01-7

ACKNOWLEDGEMENTS

My sincere thanks for all the support and help given on this venture by Dinah and David Prentice, Dr John Harcup, Peter Smith, Carly Tinkler, Ray Roberts, Brigit and Gordon Holliday, Val deHeer, Stephen Pike and David Armitage, who have also proof read and corrected my manuscript as it developed and to all those who visited my Artist's Residency in Malvern to bring me fascinating information.

Cover - Malvhina by Rose Garrard, Well Dressed 1999

Garrard Art Publications; Malvern; England

MALVERN "HILL OF FOUNTAINS"

Ancient Origins, Beliefs and Superstitions surrounding Wells and Well Dressing

LIST OF CONTENTS

Malvern May Day Festival procession 1999

The Enigma Fountain by Rose Garrard, Malvern 2000

MALVERN "HILL OF FOUNTAINS"

by Rose Garrard

DISCLOSING DIALOGUES; The Conversation

In 1992 I was invited to the Vancouver Art Gallery, Canada, as their Artist in Residence to create the next in a series of five performance installations, which I had begun in Calgary,

Alberta, two years before. As an internationally known sculptor, multi-media and performance artist living in London, I wanted to develop live works as 'conversation pieces' with communities who did not visit galleries, on issues they cared most about. Many of these people then chose to come to the gallery with objects, images and texts that represented their stories in the long display cases and I

1

translated these stories into painted images on the walls. During my work there on "Disclosing Dialogues" I was then invited to visit a native village of the Coastal Salish people on the island of Sechelt.

I was made very welcome and over tea Therese Jeffries, a Salish elder, discussed issues affecting her village, including the detrimental impact of colonialism on her childhood. Therese had been brought up by her grandmother. One morning over fifty years ago they had watched as a canoe arrived on the shore, carrying a British priest. After he was made welcome, he asked the villagers to build him a Church, when this was complete he asked them to build a schoolhouse. When this was finished he asked them to send him their children, which they did. He took the children in and closed the doors, but when the evening came they were not let out again. Her grandmother sat on the school steps wailing in sorrow every day for four months, but the children were not allowed home. Therese endured her enforced separation from her family and native language by the Catholic Church until she was twelve years old.

She showed me a photograph of her grandmother, and during this tearful encounter I apologised for the actions of my own countrymen and asked if there was any way in which I could now help. There was no direct reply, but instead Therese showed me photos of her own grandchildren and told me about life in her village during recent years. At the time I did not realise that this conversation was to change the direction of my own life in Britain.

Living at subsistence level, in about 1988 her village had been given experimental "native independence" by the Canadian Government. A national referendum on this issue was due to be held a few days after my visit, but in Vancouver

the week before, a meeting of all the Chiefs had already voted against being "given" independence in their own land. However, in the previous four years the Salish villagers had rebuilt their own homes and the long house, starting their own self-help groups for addicts and refusing all charity. The work was financed by opening a gas station and businesses that exploited the natural resources to hand, logging and dredging of gravel from the seabed. In the centre of the village, beneath taller totem poles stood a circle of faceless carved figures with a tin sign on one saying that they would only have features when the native people gained true independence. In taking responsibility on themselves, the pride and dignity of the village was also being restored. In the gentlest way I was being told that the last thing they needed was 'help' from another European.

But now with the first signs of global warming beginning to show, the foremost of their concerns was over the water rights within the reservation, which they had sold off for a large sum several years before. At the time this had seemed a good commercial deal, but the elders were starting to wonder if they had been wise. Therese said "Pure water will become the new gold of the 21st century."

I told her about Malvern, my original home town, that had been built in the 18th and 19th centuries

3

when people were attracted there by the fame of its numerous pure hillside springs. The villages of the Malverns have grown up along the flanks of the Malvern Hills, which form a boundary between Herefordshire and Worcestershire. This nine mile long range of ancient granite peaks has a necklace of springs around it, most arising where the insoluble granite meets the lower sedimentary layers of rock. Recently all Britain's water had been privatised without much opposition. I described how Malvern's water sources were taken for granted throughout the 20th century, neglected, damaged, capped and piped underground as waste-water, yet if global warming caused catastrophic flooding as some predicted, how these high springs could become lifesavers. Therese listened, looked at me long and hard and just gently said, "Go home." With this little phrase I was being reminded that this was where I had a real responsibility to offer help, in Malvern.

Malvern had been my childhood home, but I had relished leaving it for the excitement of city life in London and had never contemplated going back except for visits to family. But three years later I had bought a house here and in response to an appeal in the local press for ideas to help regenerate the town centre, by 1996 I had proposed the "Spring Water Project" to the Malvern Hills District Council. This was for a trail of sculptures by different artists on lost spring water sites throughout Malvern. In 1997 I was commissioned to do an Artist's Residency, to research spring water sites and the water trail for the Council. Throughout the two months, over one hundred pools, wells and spring water sources were mapped by local residents in my residency installation. During this, the last of five 'conversation pieces' created by me in Canada and England, Malvern people came with local objects, images and texts for the display case and told me the histories and legends connected with the wells and springs. As an artist, my long-term interests in sculpture, rituals, folk traditions, Celtic mythology, religions, feminism and ecology, were coupled with these fascinating stories, which have all inspired this small book today.

4

Artist's Residency, November 1997

Conversations with visitors

Residents map springs and wells

Sculpture " Malvhina" by the author, Well Dressed May 2000

5

I had moved my studio to West Malvern and in 1998 began work on the first sculpture, a public drinking spout that has brought spring water back to the town centre for the first time in at least thirty years.   The design of the sculpture incorporated elements representing the three springs that supply the spout, the three roads that meet here and the three most important periods in Malvern`s history, the ancient Celtic origins, the coming of Christianity and the growth of the town in Victorian times. In a Newspaper poll, a local resident suggested the spout should be called "Malvhina" after a Celtic princess who some Victorians had connected with the naming of Malvern.   In 1999 Malvhina was Well Dressed for the first time as part of the May Day Festival. The "Enigma Fountain", unveiled by Prince Andrew, followed in 2000 as the main feature on the first site of Belle Vue Island in the centre of Great Malvern, but after local elections and a change in the Council, the ten or twelve commissions planned for other artists were taken no further.

I have remained here ever since, working with others towards the rescue and restoration of Malvern`s many public and private springs. A small group of us founded the Malvern Spa Association in 1998.   In 2001 I became the organiser of the annual Well Dressing event and moved it to spring to coincide with the Malvern May Day Festival. In November 2005 I was asked to write a short article on Well Dressing and while out walking on the hills, found myself musing over the word "spring" as the name for a water source and the name for a season of the year. Searching for more information about spring rituals and their connections with springs of water, I found only scattered fragments in very diverse sources, but when I put these together they made a clearer picture of the ancient origins of Well Dressing. My article has grown into this small book, which I hope you enjoy. This is probably just a drop in the ocean of tales about Well Dressing and springtime and if you would like to tell me more, please get in touch.

ANCIENT OFFERINGS
May Day and the origins of Well Dressing

An equivalent scenario to the possible flooding effects of global warming today existed in medieval Britain, when there was little if any sanitation and sewage flowed into the nearest natural water sources. The settlements in the low-lying Severn Valley were full of the stench of pollution and disease, whilst the fame of the pure springs on the Malvern Hills spread far and wide.

"Ye nymphs, oppressed by Worcester`s stagnant air
To Malvern`s high aerial walks repair,
Where springs, and gales, their mutual aid dispense,
To purge the blood and quicken every sense."
(a poem written on a pane of glass at Malvern Wells, May 1776)

In the Malverns there are records from early medieval times to the present day of offerings and floral Well Dressings being made at several spring water sites in gratitude for this God given gift. In Greece a circular marble surround of a well or "altar" from the 2nd century BC, shows an early depiction of Well Dressing with twelve women dressing the rim by attaching ribbons to the floral garland above their heads. It was found in the sanctuary of Athena and is now in the Museum of Delphi.

Offerings of precious objects to sacred springs and wells were a common religious practice in early Roman Britain. One spectacular discovery in the bottom of Coventina`s Well near Hadrian`s Wall, was of offerings made over several centuries including

Courtesy of David Prentice

glass, pottery, goddess figures, bronzes, a human skull, plus 14,000 coins dating from pre-Roman times to the fourth century AD. When we throw coins into wells or fountains in order to be granted our wishes, we can see that the vestiges of this ancient practice are still with us today. Many tourists still throw coins into the Trevi Fountain in Rome in the hope of returning.

Victorian May Queen with retinue

The tradition of floral offerings became established in the Roman festival of Floralia on the 1st May, a celebration of Flora the goddess of fruit, flowers and fertility.   The present day crowning of a young girl with flowers as the May Queen is thought to be a remnant of this tradition. This Roman "Festival of Joy", sacred to the goddess, spread throughout their Empire and for European Christians it became the month sacred to the virgin mother Mary, when her statue is crowned and garlanded with flowers.

"Bring flowers of the rarest,
Bring blossoms of the fairest,
From garden and woodland and hillside and dale.
Our full hearts are swelling,
Our glad voices telling,
The praise of the loveliest flower of the vale.
O Mary, we crown thee with blossoms today,
Queen of the Angels and Queen of the May."

Virgin of Spain in the street

The Convent School in Worcester celebrated May in this way until at least the 1960`s, when the girls sang this special May Day hymn to Mary whilst scattering petals before her statue dressed with flowers. The verb "to dress" is defined in the dictionary as "to cleanse, to put in good order, to prepare, to make straight, to clothe, array, trim" and dressing a well was an expression of spiritual or religious beliefs that meant more than mere decoration.   By medieval times in Britain, offerings of both objects and flowers were frequently combined at May Day, when significant objects were dropped into the water to ask for a wish and garlands made of sweet smelling May Blossom were used to "dress" springs and wells in thanks for the curative powers of the pure water.

Often thought to represent the true origins of Well Dressing, the famous Derbyshire religious pictures made of panels of

petals were in fact only invented in about 1820. However the earlier tradition of Well Dressing in Derbyshire is said to go back as far as 1348 at the time of the Black Death, when pure water was endowed with special curative value.   Etwall, the

Youlgrave, Derbyshire Well Dressing 2004.   Courtesy of Edward Rokita

most recent community to take part, joined in during May 1970 and is usually the first in their Well Dressing calendar of about 100 sites to be seen in more than twenty

Courtesy of B & G Holliday

villages between May and September. Every Ascension Day
since 1845, usually in mid-May, Endon in Staffordshire has
dressed its well with flowers and since 1868 has crowned a
Well Dressing Queen as a thanksgiving for the pure water.

ANCIENT BELIEFS & SUPERSTITIONS
Fertility and Healing

But the May Day festival can be traced back to more ancient
times, when it was Beltane, the first day of Celtic summer, the
return of the sun celebrated in the hope of ensuring fertility for
the land and its people. At this time of year sources of water
were especially revered as coming from the womb of mother
earth and bringing the fertility to plants, animals and people
that was essential for their survival. Throughout Europe this
need for fertility was personified in the sculpted forms of earth
goddesses. One tiny Stone Age figure from 30,000 years ago
known as the "Venus of Willendorf", fits into the palm of the
hand like a fattened fruit, perfectly representing the fecund,

pregnant qualities that they desired
from nature. In Celtic Ireland the
sexuality of this fertility goddess was
emphasised in her frequent
representation as a "Sheela-na-gig"
displaying her genitals. This form of
goddess as sexual exhibitionist also
appears in Herefordshire beneath
the eaves of the Norman church of
Kilpeck, where she has been
interpreted as a warning to
parishioners against the temptations
of the pagan earth goddess.
Recently in the ceiling of Hereford
Cathedral the equivalent masculine
symbol of fertility was discovered,
once secretly carved on the rafters
by a medieval craftsman.

Venus de Willendorf

The survival of the Kilpeck Sheela-na-gig is remarkable as between the existing carved corbels there are a number of vacant spaces, said to have once housed other male and female fertility figures that were destroyed in the 19th century. When out walking on the hills Victorian ladies often "stoutly clutched a tall ash staff some six feet long, with a sharp iron spike on the end." *(Joseph Leech 1851)* and women were observed using these long spiked poles to chip away at the offending parts of the sculptures.   A few years

Kilpeck Sheela-na-gig

later the damaged remains were apparently removed when the church was restored.   In Ireland during the 19th century many Sheela-na-gig figures were taken from churches into the safekeeping of museum basements.   In the 1980's a student in Dublin who wanted to study these sculptures for her thesis, had great difficulty in getting permission from the museum to see them. She told me that when eventually the sculptures were shown to her, they were brought out from storage dressed in dusty babies nappies to cover their nakedness and these were removed with some reluctance by museum staff.

In an ancient British tradition that continued long after the coming of Christianity, on May Day spring water was ritually sprinkled on infertile ground and on infertile women.   In 19th century Scotland, a Mr McNeil secretly observed a fertility ritual where the stomachs, breasts and genitals of childless women were splashed in turn with water at a well.   Spring water gathered just before dawn on May Day was believed to be the most powerful to wish upon and drink, but once touched by the sun's rays its potency was diminished. Those springs on hillsides that faced the rising sun in the east were believed to be the most potent and remained the most valued.

"Those waters whose springs lie to the east are the very best of all. The waters that are exposed to the rising of the sun must needs be clear, of good smell, soft and pleasant." *(Memoirs for the History of Mineral Waters by Boyle 1815)*

Among farming communities who relied heavily on pure springs and wells, complex rituals were often performed in veneration of these water sources and in hope for the continued fertility of the land and animals. Wreaths of greenery, garlands, herbs and flowers were used to dress both people and spring water

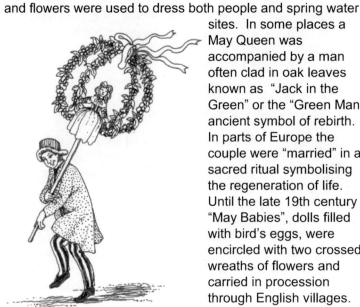

Medieval Jack in the Green

sites. In some places a May Queen was accompanied by a man often clad in oak leaves known as "Jack in the Green" or the "Green Man", ancient symbol of rebirth. In parts of Europe the couple were "married" in a sacred ritual symbolising the regeneration of life. Until the late 19th century "May Babies", dolls filled with bird's eggs, were encircled with two crossed wreaths of flowers and carried in procession through English villages.

Parading a May Baby

1950 May Queen, Angela Whithey.   Courtesy of Malvern Gazette

In the Malverns during the last fifty years the once popular customs of crowning a May King and Queen and dancing round the Maypole seem to have died out.   As a child I had watched with fascination as elaborate Celtic inter-weaves of ribbons were created by the Church School children dancing around the Maypole in the grounds of the Vicarage at St Matthias Church in Malvern Link.   Here the May Queen was sometimes accompanied by a 'Boy Bishop' wearing a mitre and the "Forget-me-not Queen" from the previous year.

In 1950 we moved briefly to Kent and my mother took me to a countryside parade of dozens of May Queens and Kings with their retinues from local village churches, who were to be judged to find the supreme May Queen.   Each group of children came in fabulous costumes of co-ordinated colours, often dressed as elves, pixies and fairies and carrying garlands of flowers.   Some 'Kings' were Robin Hood, another personification of the Green Man, and were surrounded by 'Merry Men' dressed entirely in green.

In earlier times May Blossom was gathered to welcome spring into the home. Those Hawthorn trees beside springs of water were protected from this "bringing in the May" by a curse of ill luck that would fall on those who damaged them.   The saying "Ne`er cast a clout until May is out" refers to the flowering of the May Blossom rather than the month.   Sprigs of Rowan

13

and May Blossom were also hung above entrances and laid in hearths as a protection against witches, believed to be more active on May Day. "Bel" fires were lit, two "lucky fires" and all who passed between them, particularly pregnant women and cattle, were considered cleansed and protected against the activities of fairies and witches. Celebrations continued in the fields and woods with dancing, singing and drinking, and according to disapproving clergy, were frequently followed by copulation. Their accounts became increasingly exaggerated with claims that multitudes of young girls became pregnant during May night, yet contemporary records show no related peak in the birth rate. The Church banned the 'worship' of fountains in A.D. 960 but Well Dressing itself was absorbed into the Christian tradition.

The Celtic Legacy

Several hundred years B.C. water worship had become an important and complex part of Celtic religious practice that is thought to have originated in Britain and Ireland. Druid priests are variously described in Roman accounts, from brutal and barbaric, to wise judges, philosophers and peacemakers. They carried a willow staff with which it's thought they divined water, rather like Moses in the desert, and according to Julius Caesar were respected for their study of "the stars and their motion, the extent of the world and of our earth and the 'nature of things', and the limitless power and majesty of the immortal gods."
They passed on their knowledge orally, even teaching these secrets to young Gauls sent from Europe to be educated by them, sometimes for as long as 20 years. Drawing on earlier accounts from before the 1st century B.C., Ammianus states, "The druids, men of loftier intellect, and united to the intimate fraternity of the followers of Pythagoras, were absorbed by investigations into matters secret and sublime, and unmindful of human affairs, declared souls to be immortal." It was claimed that the written works of Pythagoras originated from the oral teachings of the Druids.

King Arthur sits dying as the sword Excalibur is returned to the Lady of the Lake. Original of 14ᵗʰ century manuscript is in the British Museum.

The warrior Celts held water sources in great reverence, believing they were the source of life itself, issuing from the underworld, the entrance to the womb of mother earth. Their most precious objects, including swords, were sacrificed by dropping them into waterways, wells and pools. This ancient practice can be seen as a precursor to the romantic Arthurian legend of the return of the sword Excalibur to the Lady of the Lake. In 20th century France nearly two hundred wooden Celtic offerings carved from sacred oak were found preserved in the mud of the spring pool at the source of the river Seine. These included many carvings shaped as phalluses, "emblem of the generative power in nature" *(English Dictionary)*. Such votive offerings, including the most precious phallic symbol of power, the warrior`s sword, may have been placed in sacred water sources as ritual acts of copulation with the earth goddess and as a wish for greater potency.

But in ancient traditions, offerings to spring water sources were also often linked to a desire for healing. The Seine spring contained numerous miniature carved heads and other body parts, including limbs, torsos, eyes, breasts and small human figures showing ailments or afflictions, suggesting that the supplicants hoped to be healed. At St Thenew`s Well in Glasgow visitors used to nail up small tin shapes representing the parts of the body they wanted to have cured. Similarly, inside some European Christian churches today, those praying for a healing miracle hang miniature wax or metal replicas of the afflicted limb or body part in the chapel of an appropriate saint whose aid they seek.

The connection between springs, fertilisation and healing remained for many centuries during which more feminine sharp objects such as brooches or pins, often bent or broken as sacrifices, continued to be dropped into water sources. At the Pin Well in Northumberland there used to be a May Day procession to the well when bent pins would be dropped into the water to make wishes come true. Lovers would go to this well at midnight to offer a bent pin in the hope of a speedy and fertile marriage, but elsewhere bent pins were left to wish ill on someone. One recently recorded superstition is that two pins settling together in the water indicated pregnancy. This "offering" may be the origin of a saying still heard today, "I couldn't give two pins!" At some sites these offerings of pins were said to represent the nails used in the crucifixion and were accompanied by prayers and bible readings. Offerings of pins are significant, as until the 19th century they were precious and expensive items, which wives were often given an allowance of "pin-money" to buy.

Near Mold in Denbighshire warts were pricked with a pin, which was then dropped into the healing well to affect a cure. Suspected witches were frequently pricked with pins in search of an insensitive area or incriminating "devil`s spot" and were often ducked in water, only to be proven guilty if they floated. In Herefordshire, old Nancy Carter was mistakenly thought to have bewitched a young man and so was stuck with pins, as drawing a witches blood was thought to remove their powers. In the casting of spells, wax dolls stuck with pins were sometimes dipped in wells and hidden nearby to activate a curse. As pins pushed into a wax doll were believed to create pain, it is

Swimming a Witch,1613 Bodleian Library Oxford

possible that dropping pins into springs or wells was believed to dissolve pain. The common pain of "pins and needles" is familiar to us all and pins were evidently valued and endowed with meaning. We still say "See a pin and pick it up, and all that day you`ll have good luck. See a pin and let it lie, you`ll have bad luck until you die."

The Soul in the Skull

Historians regard the symbol of the head in Celtic worship as having held as much significance to them as the cross does among Christians today. The Celtic cult of the head was associated with water worship and both human skulls and carvings of heads have been found in their wells and pools. The Celtic legend of Bran recounts how he was shot in the foot with a poisoned arrow and realising that he was about to die, he commanded his warriors to cut off his head.   The head remained alive for 87 years, speaking, prophesying, and even after burial near London, protecting Britain from evil and

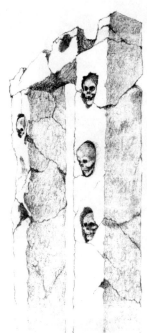

Arch of skulls found in Roquepertuse, France

invasion. The severed heads of relatives and warrior enemies alike were regarded with reverence as the sources of wisdom, prophecy and healing. The Celts believed the head contained the spirit or soul, which was immortal and would regenerate one day. These heads were not only displayed on poles in front of their dwellings as a source of protection, but also enshrined in specially carved niches in stone doorposts, as at Roquepertuse in France. They were sometimes also dropped into sacred water sources as a very precious offering to the waters of the earth mother. Perhaps this was another form of protection, consigning the souls of enemies to rot in the underworld forever, or perhaps it was so that the tribe could gain power by imbibing this "essence" of their enemies as in other cannibalistic traditions where enemy's brains were eaten.

At about the time of the birth of Christ, one account from Livy records victorious Celtic warriors drinking wine from the cleaned out skull of a slain Roman enemy and Druid priests using it in their temple as a sacred vessel decorated with gold. As Christianity took hold in Britain, the severed head remained a revered object. In Worcester the heads of the two patron saints of the Cathedral, St Oswald and St Wulstan, were encased in silver and gilt and kept as holy relics. Some ancient skulls encased in silver were deliberately destroyed as pagan relics by a medieval Bishop at St David`s in Wales. Also in Pembrokeshire, at St Teilo`s Well the custom of drinking the waters from a human skull to effect a cure had survived into the 20th century when the skull was "lost", actually sold for £50 to someone purporting to come from a museum.

corbels from 12thc. Kilpeck Church by Herefordshire School of carvers

"Green Man" heads, remains of the cloisters at Great Malvern Priory

'Celtic' head, Malvern Priory   *Site of cloisters on left of Priory*

19

As well as carving heads in wood and embossing heads on metal objects and jewellery, the Celts also carved them on to standing stones, gateposts and lintels. The first Christian chapels and the later churches followed this tradition, with heads carved on stone doorposts and arches, on ceiling bosses at rib junctions and as corbels beneath roofs. The 12th century Church of Kilpeck, built on the site of an earlier 7th century Saxon church, has some lively examples of sculpted heads as corbels by what has become known as the Herefordshire School of carvers. (See previous page)
In Great Malvern three interesting early stone heads, two "Green Man" carvings, symbols of regeneration, and one head in Celtic style were found during the building of the Abbey Hotel car park on the site of the original Benedictine cloisters and are now displayed inside a tomb recess in St Ann`s Chapel, on the south side of the present Priory Church.

In Arthurian legend the Green Knight demands that his own head is cut off, knowing he will never die no matter how often he is beheaded. This is a personification of the ancient Green Man, symbol of the immortality of nature, who seems to die each winter only to regenerate at springtime. The head of the Green Man is sometimes found carved beneath Christ`s feet on the cross as a symbol of his own resurrection from the dead. Today a sculpted head of the green man with water gushing from his mouth is a popular feature in our gardens.

Baptisms and healing

As these ancient springs were meeting places where the Celtic population gathered daily to collect water and perform Druidic rites, the first Christian "missionaries" began preaching at these sites. The Celts must have found similarities between their own beliefs and these new stories of a slain man who rose from the dead. The converts were baptised in the sparkling spring waters, which often became known for miraculous cures.

"In the course of time when the Christian Missionary came upon the scene, he preached and taught at places where men had gathered – that is, round these springs of water. Then the converts would need baptism, and so the well was made use of for that purpose, and probably its old heathen dedication was changed into a Christian one from that day onwards. As the ages went on, the memory of the holy man who had taught Christianity on any given spot was treasured up, and the well where he had given the sacrament of baptism was looked upon as something sacred. When sickness came these waters were used with faith and were said to have a healing virtue." *(Dom Ethelbert Horne c.1915)*

The first Christian chapels, churches and cathedrals were frequently built over or beside these ancient springs and wells, as at Winchester and Wells Cathedrals and with the well still inside Marden Church in Herefordshire. In 794 a miraculous spring is said to have flowed from the spot where the body of the murdered King Ethelbert was removed from this grave to Hereford.

On route a blind man accidentally touched Ethelbert's severed head and was able to see. King Offa built a church over the site of the well where "the sick were healed and the feeble minded were cured". St Ethelbert's Feast Day was the 20th May and he became the patron saint of the Saxon Cathedral in Hereford. His shrine was the focus for pilgrims until the end of the 13th century, but his head was removed to Westminster Abbey. Many of these holy water sources were said to have sprung up where a saint had been murdered, their severed head had fallen, or their body had been laid. In some places today, water from a nearby holy well is still specially brought to the church for baptisms. Even the lids of fonts in some churches were kept locked to prevent people stealing the holy water, which they believed had curative properties.

Brass of King Ethelbert in Hereford

Throughout Europe, people seeking spiritual or physical healing have bathed in or drunk from these sacred water sources, often believing that the water would respond to relevant objects dropped into its depths, or placed beside it. Since 1858, when visions of Mary led little St Bernadette to uncover a spring, pilgrims to Lourdes have sipped, bathed in and carried its holy water home with them in the hope of a cure. Today they still leave symbols of their affliction at the spring to strengthen their prayers or to demonstrate a cure.

Trees beside ancient sacred springs, particularly in Ireland and Scotland, are dressed with strips of cloth in the belief that as the cloth rots away so too the troubles of that person will disappear, but if you remove a ribbon its troubles will be yours.

There are tales of physical and spiritual retribution for those taking items left as offerings at healing wells. At tree wells these strips of cloth may originally have been used to bandage a diseased area or to clean a wound, so at very least the thief risked getting an infection. Before sunrise on May Day people

"Rag" Well Dressing of Lord Sandy's Spout, Malvern Link 2004

still gather to drink the water at the "Clootie" Well, St Mary`s near Inverness, before tying clooties to the overhanging tree to rid themselves of worries and ailments. In 1930 local charities received £24 in pennies dropped into this well on May Day, but it`s thought that they did not suffer for this removal of offerings from the well.

Well Dressing in
the Malverns

May Day revellers at Malvhina 1999

Happy Valley Donkey Spring 2005

Temperance Fountain 2004

Ariadne and the Minotaur, Lower Wyche Spout 2005

WELL DRESSING IN THE MALVERNS

Today the popularly held view is that Malvern's ancient name was Moel-bryn, meaning "bare hills", but among many other proposed origins, in 1875 James Mc Kay suggested that Malvern is pure Gaelic – Mial-chiurn – being literally "the hill of fountains or waters," pronounced as Mal-vurne.

There is now evidence for an ancient tradition of Well Dressing going back at least 800 years around this hill of fountains. In July 1870 the Malvern Advertiser stated, "Dressing wells with flowers originated in 1615 as a token of gratitude for a plentiful supply of water, when other parts of the country were suffering from the fearful effects of drought." As well as this general mention of the dressing of Malvern's wells in the 17th century, there is now evidence that at least three specific wells were also dressed in the past. Five hundred years before this there are records of offerings of thanks for the "miraculous powers" of the water being made annually at Holy Well. The Royal Well in West Malvern was regularly dressed for at least twenty years in the 19th century and the Wyche Spout was also occasionally dressed until the 1970's.

Each autumn a well decorating competition was organised by Cora Weaver on a number of sites from 1997 until 2001, when she stood down. The event had grown and was moved to May Day by the Malvern Spa Association in 2002, to become the "Wet Weekend" of Well Dressing, which I have organised since then. Hundreds of visitors come to the Malvern Hills to see about twenty four springs and wells dressed by the local community for the May Day Festival. This has revived the ancient tradition of Well Dressing in the Malverns, which can be traced back to the eleventh or twelfth century. It now also serves to increase public awareness of the dilapidated state of many of these sites, which the Malvern Spa Association aims to "conserve, protect and restore".

"O Malvern fountains pure and clear,
Each drop a glistening crystal sphere
Of priceless worth!
Let all on earth
Hold thee so dear!"
(by "a gentleman who had benefited by drinking the water", 1883)

Holy Well in Malvern Wells

Because of their healing properties and early Christian usage, many ancient sites were named as "Holy" wells and were often on the route of pilgrimage to another holy place. "We set out towards Worcester and by the way (thick planted with fruit) we deviate to the holy Wells trickling out of a Vally, thro a steepe declivity towards the foote of Greate-Maubern hills. They are said to heale many infirmities, as Kings-Evil, Leaprosie, and sore eyes." *(The Diary of John Evelyn, August 1ˢᵗ 1654)*

Remarkable cures have been attributed to this Holy Well since at least the 12th century and Nash says the spring had been "long used with great success, particularly in disorders of the eyes, scrophulos cases, old ulcers, leprosies and other

19ᵗʰ century Holy Well with baskets for carrying bottled water

Holy Well spout to be restored 2006

diseases of the skin." According to a poem in Bannister's Breviary of the Eye written in 1622, water was bottled at Malvern's holy wells and, perhaps because of the national drought of 1615, was widely distributed.

"A thousand bottles here,
were filled weekly,
And many costrils rare,
for stomachs sickly;
Some were to London sent,
Some of them into Kent,
Others on to Berwick went,
O praise the Lord."

In 1558 Queen Elizabeth I gave the well to John Hornyold and the family owned it until 1919, but the first record of a building over this site was not until 1815. The present well house was erected in 1843, based on a building in Baden-Baden, Germany, and was visited once by Princess Victoria. Until the 1960's the site became the commercial bottling plant for Cuff and Co. before it lapsed into disuse.

The Holy Well had been "standing dilapidated and slum-like" when it was bought by John and Thelma Parkes in 1970 and restored. At its reopening in 1977, Ian Masters, a thirteen-year old schoolboy from nearby Wells House School who had been suffering from a disease of the joints, reported, " My doctor said he couldn't cure it. I couldn't move my arm without it creaking. Since I bathed it in the Holy Well, it's been improving and is nearly better now."
(The Malvern Gazette, June 1977)

Frequently in medieval times, those who believed they had benefited from, or been healed by the water of a particular well or spring, would return there to make an offering. For many

Offerings, prayers and wishes left in the 'Sanctuary' room 2005

Children dress Holy Well 2000

years gifts and written prayers were left at the Holy Well in the adjacent "Sanctuary" room. Even today visitors leave objects and flowers at this well, which is now also Well Dressed every year on May Day.

"The Holy Well also appears to have been well-dressed centuries ago on the appropriate Saints Day – that of St. Oswald – when all who had been cured during the past year returned to give thanks, 'make an offering according to their substance and invoke the continuance of the miraculous powers of the well'. St Oswald was supposed to have revealed the medicinal powers of the well to one of the monks who was a hermit on the hills. ... There are stories in early books of monks wrapping cloths steeped in this water around ill patients, making them 'sleep with the wet cloths on the diseased parts'."

('What to see in Malvern' by Dr John Harcup 1975)

The St Oswald most associated with healing wells was born in A.D. 604 and was converted to Christianity at the Celtic monastery on Iona, later returning south to be crowned King of Northumbria in 633. He persuaded one of the monks, St Aidan, to found a monastery at Lindisfarne to help convert his subjects to Christianity. On witnessing Oswald`s generosity to the poor, St Aidan blessed the King's right arm making it "incorruptible". Oswald was killed in 642 during a battle near Oswestry on 5th August, now his Saints

King Oswald's head on the reliquary lid

Day, and his body dismembered. Legend has it that his constant companion, a raven, flew off with his arm to a sacred ash tree - Oswald`s Tree - and where it fell a holy well sprang up. A chapel was built over the spring and the ruins of it were still there in 1773. His severed head was recovered and taken to Lindisfarne as a holy relic and later to a new monastery at Durham where it remains inside St Cuthbert's tomb, but part of his body was buried in St Oswald's in Gloucester. A model of his severed head appears on the lid of an octagonal silver reliquary once housed in Bamburgh, Northumbria, the site of Oswald's Castle. This box set with precious gems is said to have held holy relics of the saint including his right hand that did not decay for five hundred years. (See previous page)

St Oswald's Well still exists in Oswestry and a carved head of the saint wearing a crown projected from the wall above the well until 1842 when vandals destroyed it. Those who wished to be healed would sip the water and throw the remainder over the head. The Gentleman's Magazine of 1823 recorded that "if a shirt is taken off a sick person and then thrown into this well, it will show whether the person will recover or die. If it floats it denotes recovery...to reward the saint they tear off a rag of the shirt and leave it hanging on the briars thereabouts."

But there is another St Oswald who could also be the saint celebrated at the Holy Well in Malvern. He was Oswald Bishop of Worcester and Archbishop of York, who was eventually buried in Worcester Cathedral by St Wulstan. The benevolent Oswald brought the discipline of the Benedictine Order to the secular clergy, insisting that those who served the earlier Cathedral should become monks in his new Monastery of Saint Peter in A.D. 983. He died in 992 on February 29th, now his Saints Day, and when his body was brought to be buried, a white dove hovered over

St Oswald, Bishop of Worcester

it and "a globe of fire descended on the bier and heavenly music was heard. The water with which they had washed his corpse gave sight to the blind, made the deaf hear, and the lame walk."

(The Monastery and Cathedral of Worcester by John Noake 1866)

Among many other miracles associated with his corpse over the years was the obliteration of the plague raging in the Worcester, after his body was carried around the city walls. Consequently his remains were enshrined in the Cathedral by St Wulstan in 1003. The heads of St Oswald and St Wulstan, mounted in silver and gold, became holy relics in the Cathedral and at the dissolution of the monasteries were noted in the inventory.

During the 11th century a number of monks had left the Priory at Worcester to lead a more austere life as hermits in the 'wilderness' of the Malvern Hills. Later a group of these hermits came together as a community organised by their fellow monks Eldred and Jocelin, to establish the Little Malvern Priory in 1127. The monks at Little Malvern Priory celebrated St Oswald's Feast Day during a recorded visit by Bishop Giffard in 1290, but its not known whether this

Little Malvern Priory 1808

feast day was in February or August, or for which St Oswald. But perhaps one of these monks once lived as a hermit near the Holy Well and was given this vision of its healing powers, which led to offerings of thanks for miraculous cures being made here.

31

The Wyche Well and Spout

Around the Malverns stories of herbal healers or witches abound, ranging from the play the "White Witch of Welland" to the factual accounts of 17th century witch trials recorded in the Worcestershire Sessions Rolls.

Some people assume that the area known as the Wyche Cutting, where the road cuts through the Malvern ridge, has a connection with witches and the existence of a "Pixie Path" nearby may strengthen this idea. Controversially, a wind-vane in the form of a witch on a broomstick has recently been fixed on top of the local bus shelter. Perhaps this association with witches and the supernatural that still persists today was also reinforced by stories of hangings here. After they had been  beheaded at "Sewet Oaks", serious felons were hung on the "forest gallows" at the Wyche in the 13th century and the dead bodies are said to have been carried up here along the Pixie Path.

Local legend still has it that the Pixie Path was the home of all  manner of pixies, fairies and 'little people' who only abandoned the place when quarrying began here in the 19th century. Children's fairy stories were popular fiction by this time but many eminent Victorians, including Sir Arthur Conan Doyle, continued to believe in the ancient reality of fairies. He publicly endorsed the famous Cottingley photographs of fairies taken in Yorkshire by the little sisters Elsie and Francis Wright in 1917, which were only proved to be a hoax twenty years later.

Some say that the footpath was once known as the "Pigstie Path" and was merely a very muddy pass through the hills, possibly used by wild boar or pigs. Others believe that this was a pilgrimage route through the hills and was the "Pyx Path" used by monks carrying the host from one hermit or holy place to another in a little box called a pyx. This was named after the English initials P.Y. X. derived from the appearance of the Greek "chi-rho", the sign for the name of Christ that had appeared to the Roman Emperor Constantine in a dream and was then emblazoned on his armour.

The name wyche is thought to be ancient, coming from the first settlers in the Severn vale, the Hwiccans. But the word 'wicca' meaning 'sorcerer' and pronounced 'witcha', is claimed by some not to be Celtic in origin, first appearing in a 9th century manuscript and deriving from the Old English verb "wiccian" meaning 'to cast a spell'. However, there is a link between this ancient pass and the Iron Age La Tene culture of ancient Britain who minted gold and silver coins and iron ingots as currency bars. A hoard of two hundred and fifty of these long rusty bars made from Forest of Dean iron ore was dug up in a valley above the Wyche Road in 1856 and a few of them were given to the Malvern Museum. There have been a number of other ancient finds nearby on the hill slopes.

But the word wyche may derive from the Saxon

words 'wic' meaning village, or 'wich' for a street or track often associated with salt. The Wyche Cutting is one of three passes through the hills and was probably an ancient trade route for pack animals carrying salt. Later the cutting was on one of the Roman salt trade routes from the Droit-'wich' brine springs to South Wales. In the 13th century one of these salt springs dried up but was made to flow again by a Worcestershire man, Richard of Wyche. He was later canonised and St Richard became the patron saint of the Droitwich salt trade. "Until the Dissolution, the anniversary of the saint was celebrated by the decoration or "dressing" of this (Droitwich) spring accompanied by general festivities."

(Worcestershire by L.T. Holt 1949)

During an epidemic of cholera in 1832, sufferers found the hot brine soothing and the salt waters, said to be "saltier than the Dead Sea", became famous for their healing powers. The Royal Baths were opened four years later and until recently the St Andrew's brine baths were a popular attraction at Droitwich, but were closed down in 2005.

A map of 1633 shows a spring near Wyche Cutting named as Primes Spring and earlier in about 1400 it was referred to as Primes Well, but the actual site of this well is still debated. A well is said to exist at Wyche Cutting, believed to be below ground on the corner of the rocky bank just outside the gate of High Land Cottage. After the construction of the new tarmac roadway in 1836, a public spout was installed on "the Tump" on the opposite western side of the road. In 1930 this water was described as a coming from a pure Archaean granite spring. Now named Wyche Spout, it was primarily for the use of quarrymen working for the Pix Granite Company, who lived

Well Dressing on Wyche Spout "Tump" 1978.   Courtesy of D. Beard

Wyche Spout dressed 2003

Wyche Spout dressed 2005

in the first houses built here from 1848. This spout was much valued and used by local householders until about 1990 when it was cut off as being polluted. As the water never seemed to cause them any illness, some villagers say it was cut off to deter sheep crossing the busy road from Grundy`s Meadow to have a drink, but even without the water the sheep are still a familiar sight here. The spout was Well Dressed occasionally until the 1970`s and the last known time was in July 1978 by the local newsagent Mrs Amhurst, who created a large panel of flower petals in the Derbyshire style, headed "He Giveth Water". (See previous page) The spout is now annually Well Dressed by residents who would like to see the water supply restored, which the Malvern Spa Association is working to achieve.

The Royal Well near Wyche Cutting

In 1868 a sickly William Ryland, the Mayor of Bewdley, came to Great Malvern to take the healing waters to try to cure his

Workmen posing in front of Royal Malvern Well c.1870

tuberculosis, but without success. An old resident advised him as a last resort to try the waters and air on the western side of the hills and after regularly drinking water here his health improved. The source was kept secret from him but he soon discovered the water was from St Thomas' Well inside an old cottage, which he managed to buy. But local people resented Ryland's control over the well and burnt the cottage down.

In order to placate them, in 1870 he built a public spout beside the highway, supplied from the original source and from then on villagers Well Dressed it every year with a profusion of flowers and garlands. It had been named the Royal Malvern Well by permission of Queen Victoria after her daughter Helena had visited and drunk its water. In July 1876 the Malvern News reported that the well was "beautifully dressed with flowers etc. and in the evening about twenty of Mr Ryland's tenants partook of a capital tea he had provided for them at

After drinking the Waters.

the Royal Well Brewery." A gentleman who had benefited from drinking the water from the Royal Malvern Well wrote,

"Now I saw a great crowd had surrounded the spring,
Such as might from its curative fame be expected;
Some on crutches, some each arm in a sling,
And others had bladders or kidneys infected,
Aye! all looked most miserably sad and dejected.
Lo! they drank of the nerve-bracing water designed
By Nature to strengthen both body and mind,
And rejoicing they left their disorders behind."
(Part of a poem in The Guide to the Royal Malvern Spa c. 1885)

With appeals to create a well room for the gentry, Ryland then went on to build an ambitious domed hall seating 2,000 people, "opened in May 1883 by Jenny Lind, in the greatest grandeur, before a gathering of all the Worcestershire and Herefordshire elite." *(Worcestershire Archaeology and Local History Newsletter, 1979 No 26).* This included the "Spa Pump Room", a refreshment bar, a suite of water cure baths for "tourists and invalids" and an art gallery. In a recess decorated with

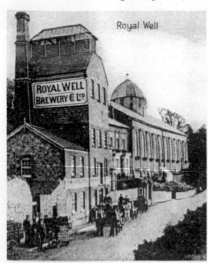

flowers was "a white marble fountain in the shape of an angel pouring water from a lily flower, which it held in the right hand, while in the left was an unfurled scroll bearing the inscription: God`s water, Drink and thirst not. Pure water is life." Behind it was a rockery with miniature cataracts supplied independently of the fountain, and in the extensive pleasure grounds outside was also a fairy grotto and fountain.

Domed hall, Royal Malvern Spa 1885

The impressive Royal Malvern Spa building was likened to St Paul`s Cathedral by the enthusiastic local press and the famous singer Jenny Lind made her last public appearance in the hall, in aid of the Railway Servant's Benevolent Fund.

By 1883 the Well Dressing event had become so popular that it had grown into a flower festival with music and tea provided for about 300 people. But in 1885 the attractive Assembly Rooms in Great Malvern were opened and the Royal Spa became known as "Ryland`s Folly", closing down in 1895. Ryland was bankrupted and the site was soon vandalised and became derelict. It was demolished in 1937, but the original Royal Well public spout remained.

In January 1970 the Herefordshire Council demolished the upper façade over the Royal Well and its royal crest and dedication stone disappeared. The spout itself was rescued from dereliction and repaired in the

1970`s, mainly through the efforts of local residents Brian Loader and Trevor Baylis, who also recovered the commemorative tablet. It was reported that "The Water Board were not in favour of restoring the water supply for public use. A grille has therefore been placed so that the water can be seen, but not reached." Trevor Baylis who had worked on the site for thirty years and run "Wyche Fireplaces" there, wrote "The well was an important part of village life as it was used for Well Dressing, which was an occasion when the local residents decorated the well with hundreds of flowers in intricate designs and during the ceremony the villagers gathered and the men drank a toast with the local beverage."

In 2005, I found another coat of arms in a local auction and this will be put back by the Malvern Spa Association as part of the Malvern`s Heritage Project springs restoration, when we hope to also restore public access to the water. The spout is now Well Dressed every year by its present owner.

Well Dressing 2005. *Courtesy C Walsh*

39

"Mother Earth" Well Dressing Evendine Spring 2004

St James' Church Spout 2005

Jubilee Fountain 2005

Well Dressing

Barnards Green Trough   2001

HIDDEN WELLS IN THE MALVERNS

The most ancient healing wells in Britain often bear the names of significant Christian figures or saints, which replaced those of earlier pagan deities. St Ann`s Well, St Agnes Well, St Thomas` Well, Walm`s Well and Moorall`s Well in the Malverns are all thought to have been named in this way and consequently would probably have been Well Dressed with offerings on appropriate religious days, even before the time of Christ.   But of these, only St Ann`s Well is still accessible to the public and so is Well Dressed today.   Other missing wells, the Hay Well and Tudor Well, have been re-discovered, Crown Stable Well has been uncovered and the waters of the Eye Well, which virtually disappeared, seem to be slowly returning.

Finding St Thomas` Well and Ryland`s Well

In 2005 Carol Walsh, the present owner of the Royal Well rang to tell me that when laying a new oak floor inside her cottage above the spout, the centre of the concrete floor underneath sounded hollow. When this area was chipped away, a covered well half full with pure, clean water, which feeds the

 public spout was revealed. It had always been rumoured that William Ryland kept secret access to a private supply from St Thomas` Well, but it was never found, until now.  The Malvern Spa Association have named this new discovery "Ryland`s Well" after its secretive founder.

This well is in turn fed by a pipe from the cottage next door and during building work there in the 1990's another well had been found, also under their front room floor. It was then covered over with glass as a 'desirable feature' and is believed to be the original St Thomas' Well, long renowned for its healing properties. There may be a Celtic connection here as St Thomas the disciple of Jesus has his Feast Day on the 21st December, the festival of the Winter Solstice on the shortest day and longest night of the year.

"In ancient deeds relating to this, The Royal Malvern Spa, it is termed 'Ye Well of St. Thomas,' and was in considerable repute even then, especially in eruptive diseases. Why the Well was dedicated to that saint, history is silent, but most medicinal springs were in a remote period of time dedicated to some saint, ...for fountains and springs were ever objects of veneration and adoration."

(Analyses of Malvern Waters by Dr S. Muspratt 1885)

But this dedication to St Thomas is probably to Thomas Cantelupe, Bishop of Hereford, who died in 1282 on the way to see the Pope in Italy because he had been excommunicated. Part of his body was buried in Orvieto but his bones and heart were brought back to the Lady Chapel of Hereford Cathedral, causing many healing miracles along the way. By 1287 his tomb was attracting so many pilgrims that in the presence of

King Edward I, it was moved to a more prominent location where those who touched it were often healed.   In the next twenty years four hundred miracles were reported here and so a papal commission was sent to Hereford to examine the truth of

seventeen of these cases. Despite being excommunicated, in 1320 the Bishop was canonised as St Thomas of Hereford and the cathedral became the most important pilgrimage site in western England. St Thomas` relics were even carried secretly though the city to heal it of the plague in the early 17th century but were 'dispersed' in the 1640`s during the Civil War.

St Thomas Cantelupe`s Feast Day is on the 2nd October and was a popular festival in Herefordshire and Worcestershire when people of all ages went 'thomasing' or asking at households for a gift, often an apple, which it was unlucky to refuse. When widows and old women knocked on farmhouse doors they were given a 'gaud', usually a measure of wheat, as a gift in memory of the saint. The tradition was accompanied by verses sung by the thomasers, a 'wassail' meaning be well, be of good health.
"Bud well, bear well,
God send spare well.
A bushel of apples to give on St Thomas` morning."
Evidently this saint was a suitable dedication for a healing well on the pilgrimage route to Hereford and it is likely that the site was Well Dressed with gifts and offerings on this St Thomas` Day in gratitude for cures here.

Walm`s Well and Moorall`s Well, British Camp

Walm`s Well, Wa`am`s Well or St Waum`s Well is at Tippin`s Rough in News Wood, on the southwestern slopes of the Malvern Hills and was named after an early Christian missionary. It is one of the most ancient surviving well sites in the Malverns, traced back to between 200 B.C. and 50 B.C., At about that time the La Tene culture of ancient Britons built a track-way to their newly fortified hilltop of British Camp, which went through News Wood and beside this well. As there were no springs within the hill defences, this may have resulted in votive offerings being dropped into its depths as in other ancient sites.

Etchings of British Camp 1817

In 1875 James McKay, a writer for the Malvern Advertiser, wrote, "In Colwall we have Walm`s Well, which yet is much resorted to by the rustics, on account of, what they regard as its admirable curative properties; and Moorall`s Well, which though less known now was formerly quite as celebrated … The Silurian Christian Missionaries Moorall and Walm stood by what we now call Burstner`s Cross and Rye Cross, endeavouring to allure the Celts from the rites and superstitions of their Druid faith. Surely we may picture woad-dyed Britons trooping from the British Camp to see little children baptised in the Gullet stream, or in the sparkling wells on the slope of the hill."

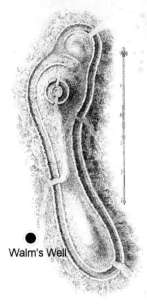

Walm's Well

From at least the 17th century Walm`s Well was revered as a healing well, particularly for skin diseases. "Walm`s well had been long used by the country people as

44

an outward application in cutaneous diseases. The water flows in a pretty copious stream and at the place where it issues from the hill, is collected by an embankment of wood and mud to form a large bath." *(Geological Essays by Mr Wallet, Surgeon of Great Malvern c.1817)* In Victorian times there was a wooden bathing hut nearby for the use of "water curists", but with only room for one person at a time.

John Masefield who came from Ledbury, claimed to have often drunk from the well in his youth as he knew of its power "to

Walm's Well below British Camp 2004   *Courtesy R Roberts*

cure broken hearts, weary eyes and rheumatism". In the 1950's he found the spring was dry, yet the well was apparently enclosed and fenced off from the public about 100 years ago as part of the privately owned Eastnor Estate. In 2004 Coca-Cola who now bottle Malvern water from Primes Well in Colwall, (known as Pewtriss Well until the 19th century), wanted to extract more water by drilling a borehole beside Walm's Well, but withdrew their planning application after it was opposed by Malvern Spa Association.

Moorall's Well

For 150 years at least there has been speculation as to the actual site of Moorall's Well or Moorally Well near Burstner's Cross, which was once the name of the road junction at the British Camp. The well was "close to the Cross Inn" and was

Burstner's Cross, British Camp Hotel & quarry.   c.1900

once described as being like the pool of Bethesda, thronged with people lying around its edges.   In 1630 Thomas Tailer, a cottager living near Burstner's Cross, dug up a beautiful gold coronet or armlet, deep set with precious gems and sold it to a goldsmith in Gloucester for £37.   This treasure may have been buried "by the British King Margadud in his flight from the Saxon leader Athelstan in pre-Roman times", but as the goldsmith broke it up to sell on the stones, we shall never know.   "Nearly two hundred years later, an urn was found in the quarry beside the same site of the British Camp Hotel.   It contained some two hundred coins, and a further search revealed a red-coloured earthen pot with another fifty coins dating from AD 286 to 311." *(Malvern Country, Vincent Waite 1968)*

Perhaps Moorall's Well was nearby and this was why these treasures were hidden here.

Today the nearest known well to the road junction is beside the British Camp Hotel in the shrubbery of Wynds Point, the former home of Jenny Lind the "Swedish Nightingale" that was built in the grounds of this quarry, but there is no evidence that this is Moorall's Well. It used to supply a public spout, still to be seen in the railings

beside the road, but sadly dry since the 1950's although now Well Dressed each year.   Perhaps Moorall's Well was in the woods across the Chase Road beside the British Camp Hotel, where in the early 20th century there was an elegant public swimming pool with a lions head water spout fed from a prolific spring.

Since the 19th century some historians have suggested that Moorall's Well was some distance away along the Chase Road. "Arthur Bennett thinks it springs from a little above the western boundary fault … and three quarters of a mile south-south-west of Wyche Cutting. There used to

Public Swimming Pool, British Camp Hotel, 1920's

47

be a cottage here with a bath 'lined with bricks'."
(Wells & Springs of Worcestershire, HM Stationery Office 1930)

It was famed for healing eye diseases and so is also said to have been on the western end of the same fault line as Eye Well and Holy Well on the other side of the hills. "It is situate on the western side of the hill, directly opposite to the holy well. There is also a bath and a cottage near it ; formerly there was a bath lined with bricks in this tenement, but it is at present filled up. We understand however, it is in contemplation to restore this bath to its original state for the use of the public." *(History of Malvern by J. Chambers 1817)*

In "Aquae Malvernensis" Cora Weaver and Bruce Osborne deduce from early maps that Moorall`s Well is actually Pitt`s Spring near the Kettle Sings café, "on the bend in the road midway between Ballards Spring and Gardiners Common", but now only "a small streamlet running alongside the road and a cistern in the garden of Box Cottage." This would suggest that yet another of Malvern`s ancient healing wells has come to a sorry end.

TALES OF SOLITARY MONKS AND HERMITS

Many solitary monks and hermits were said to people caves on the lower slopes of the Malvern Hills by the eleventh century, each living a life of poverty, chastity and obedience beside one of the prolific springs or wells.
 "Aged the sires who dwelled such caves within-
Head-shaking sages prone to moralise
And him disciple, who made here his inn.
Their cheeks were hollow, slender was their size,
And ever on the ground they bent their eyes.
One book they had - the book of holy lore,
Against the wall the cross stood leaning-wise.
A table small, a skull and cross-bones bore,
And bosky ivy hid the bell above the door."
 (The Monastery and Cathedral of Worcester by John Noake 1866)

Legend has it that one hermit lived in "Clutter's Cave" above Walm's Well, possibly another in "The Hermitage", now a cottage, near the spring on Westminster Bank in West Malvern at that time owned by the bishopric of Westminster. A third hermit inhabited a cave, long since collapsed, at Ivy Scar Rock near the spring and a fourth, a monk called Werstan apparently lived first in a small cave and spring in the Holly Mount Wood, now above Holly Mount Church in Great Malvern.

St Werstan's Well?

Having fled an invasion by the Danes at Deerhurst Abbey near Tewkesbury, the Abbot Werstan was "guided by angels" to build a little oratory, - a Chapel to St Michael,- on a narrow

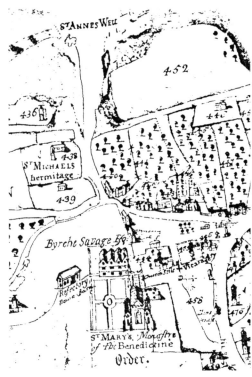

terrace below St Ann's Well. In 1544 Richard, Robert and Roger Taverner were noted as buying "Saint Myghelles chapel, with its garden, beneath le Malvern Hyll". The building was marked on a plan of Malvern in 1725 by Joseph Dougherty and was again recorded on his 1744 map as St Michael's Hermitage. Eighty years later when a cottage called "the Hermitage" was demolished on the site, a small crypt containing human bones was found beneath it. But as it was reported that the crypt also held encaustic tiles, said to have been like those from the 15th century in the present Priory, its earlier origins are in doubt. Also no written record of Werstan appears before the dissolution of the Monasteries by Henry the Eighth. Only in 1465 was Werstan portrayed in the stained glass windows of the newly rebuilt Priory as "St Werstan" the martyr, with swordsmen striking his head as he leans out of the Chapel window. As no such saint appears in the Christian Calendar some historians question both his martyrdom and even his existence.

But this crypt is still thought to exist near the house named "Bella Squardo" at the top of the Ninety-Nine Steps. Beside the house there was an old donkey stable, said to have been built in about 1820. In the 1970`s the then owner, Phillip Evans, took up the floor and found two early unmarked stone slabs which he put in the garden. It is known that sometimes a hermit or monk chose to sleep on a stone slab, but Mr Evans described these as "coffin lids". As his spade often hit other solid flat surfaces in the garden, he suggested that the area might have other burials in it and could have been a graveyard for the monks.   When digging here he also uncovered a large quantity of broken pottery shards, but these

Possible site of St Michael's Chapel.
Rose Bank Gardens & Bella Squardo

15th century encaustic
tiles, Gt Malvern Priory

Site of donkey stables, now garages, where 'coffin lids' were found

were probably from the Muriel Lanchester Pottery here in the
1940`s, as there were no encaustic tiles amongst them.
Today two garages occupy this site but behind them is another
building once used by Mr Evans as workshops, now converted
into a separate house called "Halfway" where an old well was
found beneath the present hallway.   Looking at the early

maps, St Michael's Hermitage may have been on the next small terrace below here, now part of the publicly owned Rosebank Gardens where there are several underground water sources. If Werstan was here, the existence of a well makes more sense of his choice of this site, suggesting that he may not have had to make the steep daily climb up to St Ann's Well to fetch water.

Hay Well and St Agnes Well

But Aldwin, an unlettered man who had been made a monk by St Wulstan the last Saxon Bishop of Worcester, was sent to live in this dense forest 'wilderness' landscape populated by wild boar and wolves. After several years in uneventful isolation, he and a companion called Guy sought adventure, returning to the Bishop to ask if they might "either see the tomb of our Lord, or perish happily by the hand of the Saracens" in the Holy Land. The Bishop refused their request and persuaded Aldwin to return, as "God would work great things in Malvern". This prediction came true. Aldwin attracted thirty other hermits to join him and in 1085 founded the Benedictine Priory dedicated to St Mary, on the flatter land below St Michael's Chapel. The Priory was later dedicated to both saints.

The spring water that must have originally sustained him as a hermit was most probably supplied from a cluster of sources now hidden at the bottom of the Haywell Steps behind Warwick House in Great Malvern. Perhaps he quenched his thirst with the water from the Hay Well, piped later to supply the Benedictine Priory buildings, or from the pool in a forest clearing here that was fed by the Hay Well, or from the nearby St Agnes Well. "Hay" is the Anglo Saxon word for an enclosure or forest clearing for animals and 18th century maps show the Hay Well above a pond in South Field, just such a clearing not far from the Priory.

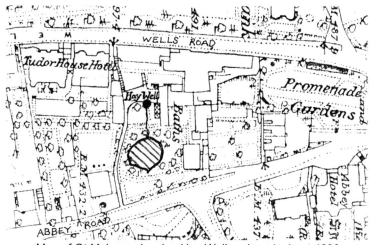
Map of Gt Malvern showing Hay Well and pool, about 1890

"On the other side of the road and at the end of a little walk, hid away under some wet haired willows, is the Hay Well, the most abundant of the many springs that come oozing and bubbling out of the bowels of the Malvern Hills. It is a round basin, some five or six feet deep, about the circumference of a cart-wheel, and like a punchbowl in everything but the potency of the beverage it contains."

(Three Weeks in Wet Sheets by Joseph Leech 1851)

The ancient Hay Well and St Agnes Well are sadly now both covered over by a driveway and car park belonging to the Baptist Church built in 1894. In the 1960's the rim of the Hay Well was briefly uncovered beneath concrete foundations during building work, but the waters can be heard and glimpsed flowing underground from a tank behind the Church. The water still feeds a pool, now shrunk to the garden pond of the Salisbury, formerly Font Hill House, where in 2003 medieval stonework was found with a group of old bones that were taken away by the police for forensic testing, but no more was heard of them. In 1997 water diviner Peter Ewence dowsed the flow downhill with me, to where it emerges in Priory Park as a tiny crescent shaped pool, then as the

Pond in the garden of the Salisbury

Hay Well rim uncovered in the 1960's.   Courtesy of Dr John Harcup

Peter Ewence dowsing Hay Well 1997

Site of St Agnes Well

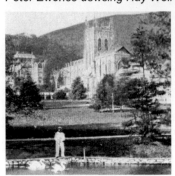

Swan Pool Priory Park 1920

Crescent pond Priory Park

ornamental stream, which in turn feeds the lake of Swan Pool, originally the Benedictine Priory fish pond.

St Agnes Well is probably "older than the Hay Well and may have been the source of the domestic supply to the farm buildings which existed on the site of the present Baptist Church." *(Worcestershire Wells and Springs, H.M. Stationery Office 1930)* St Agnes dedicated herself to Christ, refusing to marry and was martyred in Rome in about A.D. 305, aged only thirteen. St Agnes is associated with farms as her emblem is a lamb, from "agnus" meaning lamb and because she was sacrificed like a lamb by her throat being cut. Her feast day is 21st January, when in Rome lambs are still blessed and their wool used to weave robes for archbishops by the nuns of St Agnes Convent.

Recently, in redevelopment work at the back of the Warwick House site an early ditch was excavated, but not to the bottom of the feature, presumably because time was limited. The lowest uncovered deposits were dated to the 13th or 14th century and contained numerous fish bones including, fresh water eel, pike, chubb and gudgeon, and sea herring, plus wild rabbit and fallow deer. Bones of animals thought to have been farmed here, included beef, lamb, pork, geese and chicken, and there were also many eggshells.
"A concentration of such waste is rare and is most often associated with large, well organised estates or large urban centres, usually of medieval or post-medieval date. …
Fishponds were expensive to maintain and were therefore only associated with wealthy or well-organised institutions."
(Archaeology Service of Worcestershire County Council, 2004)

In 2005, after holding a workshop with the Malvern Spa Association, Peter Golding from the Water Divining Group of the British Society of Dowsers wrote, "Near the Baptist Church, organiser Rose Garrard asked if we could locate the position of two lost wells, Hay Well and St Agnes Well. Rowan Thompson and I had soon dowsed and agreed the location of both and identified which one had been known as St Agnes

Well. "Was it a public well?" was my question, "Yes, but..." the rods indicated. So perhaps it wasn't officially available. "Did the public use it?" "Yes!" At that moment a resident of Warwick House leaned over his fence to say "If you`re looking for a well you are on the right spot. A few months ago the wheel of a lorry sank into it!" "

In the 1840`s, the early St Agnes Well was contained inside a new building, the Haywell Baths, a private development only for the use of hydrotherapy patients taking the "Water Cure" with Dr Gully. Soon the unusually warm water of the nearby

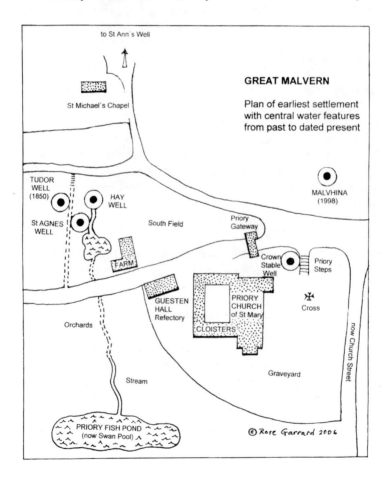

Hay Well also became unavailable to the general public, after it was covered over and piped to several nearby premises. The Malvern Advertiser implied some criticism of this commercial development in 1877.

"The Hay Well, situated in the centre of the town, might have become a central attraction had the same spirit actuated the Malvernians that actuated the people of other watering places...where a spring would be so conducted under an imposing artistic canopy, that it would become a favourite lounging place for visitors and another item of interest." Eventually the bathhouse was demolished, but the wells remain, still hidden below ground in the centre of Great Malvern.

From these two 'missing' wells we begin to get a picture of the first settlement of Malvern; a small farm beside a forest clearing where sheep graze, providing wool for the clothing of the monks in the nearby Priory, meat for their table, plus fish on Fridays caught in their own fish pond and pure well water to drink. In "The Spring Water Project" report to the Council in 1998, I proposed that these wells were at least identified and marked by ornamental cover plates, in a similar way to the Chalice Well at Glastonbury. These covers were to be commissioned from a local craftsperson, but as the newly elected Malvern Hills District Council took the idea no further, these two historically important wells that enabled the founding of Great Malvern remain invisible.

Tudor Well in Great Malvern

The town of Great Malvern grew up during the 18th and 19th centuries as the fame of its healing water sources spread and were then commercially exploited by Doctors Wilson and Gully, who had brought the Priessnitz water cure here from Graefenberg, Germany. Rather too late for Prior Aldwyn to have drunk from it, the Tudor Well, the third and most recent

TUDOR HOUSE HOTEL,

well in this cluster round Haywell Walk, was created over a prolific spring discovered in about 1850 in the garden of Hollyrood House and the Tudor Hotel owned by Dr Gully. Whilst excavating the site to install a gas supply to light some of the nearby premises, "a large spring of water suddenly burst into an opening the workmen were then sinking. The rush of water was so great that pumping operations were for a time resorted to ... The spring proved to yield a never failing supply of good water... so that the proprietors thought it well to abandon the gas works in favour of the water."

(Brief of Evidence to House of Lords by Mr Hillyard 1905)

The Tudor Well supplied about 20,000 gallons a day and was contained in a separate Victorian bathhouse for the use of

patients who came to stay in Malvern to take the Water Cure with Dr Gully. The bathhouse had been demolished by the 1960's, but until recently the well was owned by the Severn Trent water company. The well site has just been bulldozed for a carpark and the neglected well is derelict, hidden under rubble and rubbish just behind the boundary wall. The Tudor Well Warden and the Malvern Spa Association have tried to save this site and have now been assured that the well itself will be kept by the developer.

Uncovering Crown Stable Well

A third possible, but least likely source of water for Aldwyn could have been the well in the old cellars still beneath the shops on the Priory Steps. This well was first reported to me in 1997 by Mrs Hunt who was once the proprietor of Tipping and Morris' wine shop above the site and whose husband, a marine, had then lifted the heavy slab that covered it.

In 2004 John Bibby from the Malvern Spa Association created an ingenious pulley system attached to the ring in the large flagstone, to reveal this beautiful circular well once more. The actual age of this well is not yet known, but Roger Hall-Jones from nearby printers First Paige, has some original deeds from 1833 when their premises were the stables for the nearby Crown Hotel built in about 1753. This building was leased by

Dr Wilson and Dr Gully as the first "Water Cure" establishment, which they renamed "Graefenberg House" in 1842 and is now Lloyds Bank. These documents state that the owner of the premises that were the stables still has the right to draw water from this well. Although public access to this well is restricted, the Malvern Spa Association hope that it can be Well Dressed at May Day in future years.

Eye Well above Malvern Wells

"A little more I`ll of their curing tell,
How they help sore eyes with a new-found well;
Great speech of Malvern Hills was lately reported,
Unto which spring people in troops resorted."
('Breviary of the Eye' by Richard Bannister, 1622)

Another famous Malvern water site is the Eye Well, now only a
tiny bubbling pool of water above the Holy Well, but long
renowned for its healing of diseased livers, kidney stones and
other ailments as well as eyes. "Eye Well is a spring that has
been long famed for the virtue of healing eyes and other parts
of the head." *(Camden`s Britannica By Dr Hopkins c. 1817)*

According to a Mr Wickham, the Eye Well was a much more
prolific source until the 19th century, when seeking to pipe the
water to his home, a local resident struck the ground with a
pick axe only to see the water disappear completely.
"Mr Bennett says that owing to such experiences owners of
springs in Malvern are always very careful how they interfere
with springs. It is the brashy nature of Malvern rock which
causes such an occurrence." The Eye Well later reappeared.
"The water oozes out of the Archaen rock, but owing to the
path functioning as a dam the 'well' is now simply a little
morass." *(Wells & Springs of Worcestershire 1930)*   A little more of
the water seems to have returned and this spring is now
regularly cared for and dressed annually by its Malvern Spa
Association Well Warden who lives nearby.

In the 18th century Dr John Wall analysed the purity of
Malvern`s spring waters when treating his patients at
Worcester Infirmary and developing English bone china in
Worcester, now Royal Worcester Porcelain. The profits from
his book "Experiments and Observations on the Malvern
Water" published in 1756,
"were devoted to assisting the many needy sick who came for
treatment." *(F.C. Morgan, Public Librarian, Malvern c.1930)*

*Portrait of Dr John Wall with his Worcester Porcelain in foreground.
Courtesy of Rt. Hon. Lord Sandys*

Well Dressing, Eye Well on hills above Holy Well, 2004

He also raised subscriptions from the gentry to make the springs "more commodious" for the public. At a time when the level of the unpleasant taste of minerals in waters was believed to signify their power to heal, Dr Wall promoted the unusually clean taste and purity of Malvern water as its healing power and this attracted many famous people to the town. He is popularly remembered in the rhyme,
"The Malvern water, says Dr John Wall,
is famed for containing just nothing at all."

Among the many healing wells, the most commonly claimed cures seem to be for complaints affecting the eyes. A woman with her eyes so inflamed that she could not see, went to this respected physician. "He advised her to visit the Eye Well and following a week of bathing her eyes in its water her sight was 'so much recovered that she could see a Flea leaping on her bed'." *(Dr John W. Harcup, 'The Malvern Water Cure' 1992.)*

But the reasons for these cures caused some debate between the scientific and religious community. In about 1915 Dom

The Eye Well waters are slowly returning

Ethelbert Horne wrote, "... so it was by these waters that the recipient came out of the blindness of heathenism into the light of faith. This spiritual sight which baptism was said to give to the soul was taken, as time went on, to mean sight to the eyes, and hence rose the common belief in the efficacy of the water from these wells for all complaints which affected the seeing."

GRANDMOTHER GODDESS
St Ann's Well above Great Malvern

In an attempt to supersede the pagan beliefs of Britain, Christian Saints were often named as the guardians of many of these springs and wells, replacing the names of earlier pagan deities. One of the most popular dedications was to St Anne, patron saint of springs, whose many wells can be found across the country. In Worcester her feast day was celebrated at the Cathedral as early as the time of Bishop Simon, between 1125-1150. The original St Ann's Well cottage in Malvern dates from 1813 and it soon became a popular spring used by people taking the Water Cure. Schweppes bottled water here for a number of years as it was claimed to be "the purest natural water in the British Isles".

From 1815 the Clifton family lived in the well cottage, renting it for five guineas a year from the Foley Estate. Hester, "a very upright and correct lady", her husband John and her daughter

St Ann's Well in about 1820 showing small bathhouse on lower left

63

Mary, supplied water cure visitors with refreshments in the "Tea Gardens" and with hot and cold baths in a nearby small building. In 1826 Hester died, but John lived on for a further twenty years until he was ninety. Mary ran the business until her own death in 1860, the same year that the octagon was probably built. The 1851 census records the presence of Mary's young niece and Elizabeth a servant, appropriately named Drinkwater, who may have been working there.

Joseph Leech described the well room in 1851 in his satirical book "Three Weeks in Wet Sheets by a Moist Visitor". "The water itself, which dribbles away into a carved stone basin at the rate of about a glass a minute, through a kind of penny whistle placed in the mouth of a pleasant dolphin, is quaffed by crowds in a little house which is half a peddlar's shop and half a pump-room, attached to a cottage where knives and

A DRINK AT ST ANNE'S WELL.

forks are hired out to tourists, and kidneys surreptitiously grilled between meals for hungry patients under water treatment." The site is now Well Dressed annually by staff at the present St Ann's Well Cafe.

The first mention of St Ann's Well was by the Bishop of Westminster in 1282 and appears in the parish records, but the origins of both the well and the name Ann are thought to be much earlier than that. St Anne herself was the apocryphal grandmother of Jesus, appearing first in the 2nd century writings of James as mother of the Virgin Mary.

She is said to have given birth to many Saints and became the patron Saint of midwives. But Anne's name corresponds with the names of earlier grandmother fertility goddesses across Europe and the Middle East. Long before the bible was written, in Syria she was the Grandmother Goddess known as Anatha, in Canaan as Anat and in Sumeria she was already known as Anna the Grandmother of God. In Semitic texts she was Di-Ana or "Goddess Anna", and as Anna Perenna she was the Roman's "Grandmother Time". The Celtic tribes were ruled by her as Ana or Anu, first of the female trinity of the

Chakra Points superimposed on the 500 ft contour line of the Malvern Hill range

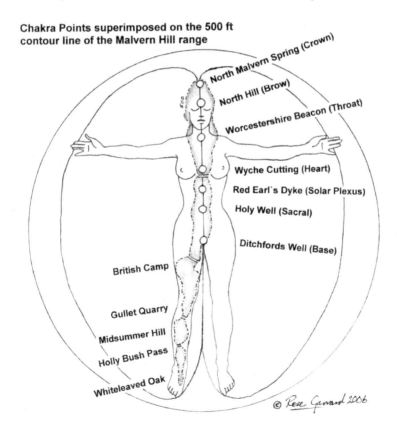

North Malvern Spring (Crown)

North Hill (Brow)

Worcestershire Beacon (Throat)

Wyche Cutting (Heart)

Red Earl's Dyke (Solar Plexus)

Holy Well (Sacral)

Ditchfords Well (Base)

British Camp

Gullet Quarry

Midsummer Hill

Holly Bush Pass

Whiteleaved Oak

© Rose Garrard 2006

65

The hills as the sleeping Goddess, Well Dressing 2004

Morrigan, associated with rebirth and regeneration. Anu was the "divine mother" of early pagan Ireland, her name, which also means treasure, wealth and plenty, was given to two hills in County Kerry called the "Paps of Anu". The contours of the landscape were regarded as the body of the mother goddess, the hills representing her breasts in County Kerry, and her womb at Silbury, Wiltshire.

Today the range of the Malvern Hills is believed by some local people to represent the sleeping earth goddess, with St Ann`s Well nestling between her breasts. The Gatekeeper Trust who

organise regular pilgrimage walks, have identified a line of Chakra points along her body, the hills. (See previous page) The Celts believed that the mother goddess was the source of all water issuing from the earth or from her vagina, sacred waters conveying fertility and giving birth to all living things. At St Anne`s Well in Llanmihangel, South Wales an ancient carved bust of the Saint still "issues water from her nipples and vagina".

St Ann`s Well Restoration

On December 9th 2005 at noon, a happy crowd of about a hundred people gathered in the courtyard of St Ann`s Well to celebrate the completion of work on this, the first of fourteen spring sites to be restored as part of the Malvern`s Heritage Project financed mainly by the Heritage Lottery Fund. The three spring water outlets at St Ann`s Well had all been dressed with flowers and garlands by members of the Malvern Spa Association, and while everyone supped a glass of port and a mince pie, beautiful harp music was played from the octagon balcony by Jonathan Penley.

The oval pond and cascade, side spring and trough, and terraces with new "fern" benches had all been restored in a unique partnership between the Malvern Spa Association, the local Area of Outstanding Natural Beauty office and the land owners Malvern Hills Conservators who also contributed to the finances. Speeches introduced us to those organisations and individuals who formed the vital background support to this event and Jonathan then sang an 18th century poem about Malvern water, which he had set to music.

"Oh Malvern, never envy thou
  the springs enroled by fame
since Wall`s ingenious pen has now
  immortalised thy name.
Henceforth shall rapturous poets sing
  of Helicon no more;
the waters of thy purer spring
  can boast superior power.
We too of inspiration tell,
  as bards who drink shall feel,
the streams from Malvern`s holy well
  can both inspire and heal."

(Worcester May 1755, Hydropota)

St Ann's Well restoration 2005

Well Dressing
Malvern's Heritage Project

Building 'Old Moses Trough'

St Ann's Well
Restoration

Harp music from the balcony

Naming Old Moses Spout

A donkey called Emily stood patiently by while these celebrations were taking place, to remind us of the historic role of these hard-working animals at St Ann's Well. But to everyone's amusement, she stubbornly refused to drink from the side spring, thought to have been the watering place for donkeys that used to carry visitors up the steep hill. Donkeys had been a popular way of ascending the hills since before 1817 and by 1852 there were ten donkey-hire stands in Great Malvern alone. Just one old wooden stable now remains, at the bottom of Happy Valley. Restored as a cascade and animal trough, the spring was blessed by Reverend John Barr from Malvern Priory and newly named "Old Moses Spout" by Anne Jenkins of the Heritage Lottery Fund in memory of one particular donkey.

Local people still recount the story of "Old Moses", a donkey owned by Betty Caley in the mid 19th century, who they say once carried Princess Victoria up to the well. Moses seems to have been very popular and was portrayed as an aging donkey affectionately called "Old Moses" in an engraving of 1855.

OLD MOSES

"In 1831, the Duchess of Kent brought the young Princess Victoria, then twelve years old, to stay at Hollymount Cottage for several months. Here the child rambled freely in the woods and on the hills, and rode often on the donkeys, especially her favourite Moses, who thereafter was called the "Royal Moses", attended by the donkey-woman in a bonnet and red cloak. ...She (Princess Victoria) performed here what was probably her first public function by declaring open a new path made near St Ann`s Well, from Nob`s Delight to the Foley Walk." (called Victoria Walk) *(A Little City set on a Hill by C.F. Severn Burrow 1948)*

Group of Donkey Women Malvern

In his book "Malvern Country", Vincent Waite says, "For many years one of the Malvern Donkeys bore a badge of distinction on its bridle and was given the name 'Royal' Moses as a reward for carrying the future Queen of England up to the top of Worcestershire Beacon." The publicity created by these royal events made Malvern a most elegant and fashionable resort, attracting well-to-do visitors at least ten years before the expensive "Water Cure" treatments of Dr Wilson and Dr Gully had begun.

MAKING A BARGAIN FOR DONKEYS.

In his guide to Malvern in 1894 Charles Grindrod records that another royal, Queen Adelaide, often visited Malvern and when staying at Witley Court in 1843

Master H.& the Nonimus Minstrels   *Emily the donkey centre stage*

St Ann's Well Celebrations 9th December 2005
Malvern's Heritage Project financed by HLF & MHC

*Sarah Falkland from BBC TV, tries to position a reluctant Emily in
front of the celebratory crowd at the opening of the restored well*

she also enjoyed riding the hills on Moses. Grindrod says it was Queen Adelaide who renamed him as "the Royal Moses", but whatever the case, those wanting to emulate these royal journeys sadly soon rode him to death. Afterwards many of the local donkeys were renamed Royal Moses in his memory, but others say it was only to try to attract more customers!

In 2005 a BBC television news team covered the celebration of St Ann's Well restoration, which merrily concluded with some verses from a 17th century song extolling the healing properties of Malvern water, probably written by the then Vicar of Malvern. Sir Edward Elgar had set these verses to music when he lived in Malvern and sent the score to his friends as a Christmas card in 1897. Especially for this celebration, those verses praising Malvern water had again been set to music, but now as "Malvern Rock" composed and performed by Master H. and the Nonimus Minstrels.

"Great Malvern on a rock, thou standest surely;
Do not thyself forget, living securely;
Thou hast of blessings score,
No country town hath more,
Do not forget therefore,   To praise the Lord.

Out of thy famous hill, there daily springeth
A water, passing still, which always bringeth
Great comfort to all them
That are diseased men,
And makes them well again. To praise the Lord.

Hast thou a wound to heal, the which doth grieve thee?
Come then unto this well, it will relieve thee;
`Noli me tangeres`,
And other maladies,
Here have their remedies, Prais'd be the Lord."

THE CYCLE OF REGENERATION
The Masculine and Feminine Landscape

The Celtic year began on 1st November at the onset of winter, with the fire festival of Samhain during the previous night, when all old fires were extinguished and new ones lit from beacons kindled by the Druid priests to repel evil spirits. These fires cleansed the community of past ills, celebrating the death of the old, reflected later in All Souls Eve, and the

A beacon lit to celebrate the marriage of Earl Beauchamp July 1902

regeneration of a new cycle of life. Roman records claim that the Celts sometimes burnt live human and animal sacrifices contained in wicker cages as offerings at this time. In 1874 Queen Victoria had an "immense" bonfire lit in front of Balmoral Castle on this Halloween night, with people dressed as fairies escorting the effigy of a witch to be burnt on the fire. Until the beginning of the 20th century some places still lit huge hilltop fires at Samhain, but since the Gunpowder Plot of 1605 these have been gradually replaced by the bonfires of

Preparing a bonfire on the Worcestershire Beacon 1863

November 5th and the burning of the "Guy", an effigy of the plotter Guy Fawkes.

St Ann is often associated with flattened hilltops lit by beacons, from the similar Celtic word "tan" meaning fire or beacon. "Tan hill, Tan Woods and Tan Fields abound in parishes around Malvern…It was easy to change Tan Hill to St Ann`s Hill and to divert to a Catholic Saint the miraculous powers attributed to the Celtic fire-god." *(Norman May`s Guide to Malvern 1886)*

During his search for 'ley" lines in the landscape of Britain, Alfred Watkins of Hereford observed, "The ley line terminates in the highest hill on the Wiltshire Downs, Tan Hill, and tan in modern Welsh means "fire," although corrupted here to St Anne`s Hill. … It seems very evident that the direction of sunrise on one day in the year, not being a convenient standard for other times, there were established sun substitutes, beacon lights on the ley."
(The Old Straight Track by Alfred Watkins, 1925)

Some historians claim that the well in Malvern was not named after St Ann until the mid-eighteenth century, though others

claim this earlier Celtic past
with its links to fire, beacons
and the sun.
"St Ann`s Well - in its primary
form means simply "the well
dedicated to the sun."
*(The British Camp by James
McKay 1875)*

Evidence of an ancient fire
ritual has been found on the
Worcestershire Beacon. A
bronze-age cremation burial of
an adult with a distinctive
pottery 'pygmy' cup or urn
dating from between B.C.1600
to 760 was uncovered on the
very top of this hill in November
1849. A mapping survey was
being undertaken by the Royal
Ordnance Corps and a Private

Victoria's Golden Jubilee 1887

Harkin was excavating to find the trigonometric marker stone
from a previous survey. He firstly uncovered part of a human
skull and then, "On uncovering the rock, about nine inches
below the surface, just on the outer edge, the small urn was
found in a cavity of the rock, with some bones and ashes. The
urn was placed in an inverted position, covering part of the
ashes. …The conspicuous position of the site where this

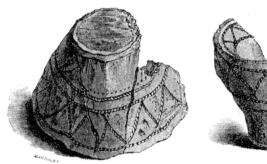

Pymgy Cup from the Beacon c.1000 B.C. Courtesy of Dr J Harcup

75

deposit was found, being the highest point of the hill range in the part adjoining Great Malvern, seems to indicate that it was the resting place of some chieftain or person of note at an early period in our history."

(Antiquities & Folklore of Worcestershire by Jabez Allies 1852)

Many beacons have been lit on this hilltop since then, but to celebrate the marriage of Prince Charles and Diana in 1981, a beacon was deliberately sited exactly over the trigonometric point, the site of this ceremonial fire 3000 years ago.

It is no mere coincidence that the well of St Ann above Great Malvern nestles beside the flat promontory of St Ann`s Delight and below this ancient hill where beacons are still lit.

Fire substitute for the sun on Worcestershire Beacon This windy site brings together the elements of earth, fire and water in symbols, both for the phallus - here a fire-god as the beacon substitute for the sun, - and the womb as the waters of the oval pool of an earth goddess. Both are as old as the oldest civilisation, or "as old as the hills" and even today we are influenced by their ancient story. Perhaps when we lie in the sun to get a "tan" and call our

The restored oval pool of St Ann's Well 2005

own grandmothers "Nan" or "Nana" we will be reminded of these ancient origins, beliefs and superstitions.

The end is just the beginning in the cycle of regeneration, likewise in this little book and with the Well Dressing of this, the first restored spring in Malvern`s necklace of one hundred springs around the hill of fountains, St Ann`s Well.

St Ann's Well nestles between Worcestershire Beacon and North Hill

Bibliography
FURTHER READING

1817 History of Malvern by John Chambers, Longman, Hurst,
 Rees,Orme and Brown
1851 Three weeks in Wet Sheets by a Moist Visitor (Joseph Leech)
1852 Antiquities and Folklore of Worcestershire by Jabez Allies
1866 The Monastery & Cathedral of Worcester by John Noake
1875 The British Camp by James McKay, Malvern Advertiser
c. 1885 Guide to the Royal Malvern Spa, Hall, Art Gallery and
 Pleasure Grounds
1886 Norman May`s Guide to Malvern
1901 The Malvern Country by Bertram Windle, Methuen & Co.
1914 Great Malvern Priory Church by Rev. Anthony C. Deane, Bell &
 Sons
1925 The Old Straight Track by Alfred Watkins, Methuen & Co Ltd
1930 Worcestershire Wells and Springs, His Majesties Stationary
 Office
1948 A Little City set on a Hill by C.F. Burrow, Priory Press, Malvern
1949 Worcestershire by L.T. C. Rolt, Robert Hale Ltd
1958 The Herefordshire School of Sculpture by F. C. Morgan
1961 Kilpeck Church by C. Winsor Richards, E. N. Hillier & Sons
1964 A History of Malvern by Brian S. Smith, Leicester University
 Press
1968 Malvern Country by Vincent Waite, Aldine Press for J.M. Dent &
 Sons
1970 Customs and Folklore of Worcestershire by Lavender M. Jones,
 Estragon
1974 Folklore and Customs of Rural England by Margaret Baker
1976 Fairs and Revels by Brian Jewell, Midas Books
1982 Earth Rites by Janet & Colin Bord, Granada Publishing
1985 Guide to Traditional Customs of Britain by Brian Shuel, National
 Trust
1986 The Celts by Frank Delaney, Hodder and Stoughton
1986 Woman's Encyclopaedia of Myths & Secrets by Barbara Walker,
 Harper Row
1987 Ancient Mysteries of Britain by Janet & Colin Bord, Paladin
1989 The Once and Future Goddess by Elinor W. Gadon, Harper
 Row
1990 Sacred Places by James A. Swan, Bear and Company
1991 The Myth of the Goddess by Anne Baring & Jules Cashford,
 BCA / Penguin
1992 The Malvern Water Cure by John Winsor Harcup, Winsor Fox

Photos

1992 The Folklore of Hereford & Worcester by Roy Palmer, Logaston Press

1993 Not the Least, the Story of Little Malvern by Ronald Bryer, Hanley Swan

1994 Archiving My Own History by Rose Garrard, Cornerhouse Gallery, Manchester

1994 Aquae Malvernensis by Cora Weaver & Bruce Osborne, Cora Weaver

1996 Stations of the Sun by Ronald Hutton, Oxford University Press

1997 The Earth Goddess; Celtic and Pagan Legacy of the Landscape, Blandford

1998 The Water Wizard by Viktor Schauberger, Gateway Books

2005 Images of England ; The Malverns by Brian Iles, Tempus